THE LEWIS AND CLARK TRAIL

Then and Now

The Lewis and Clark TRAIL Then and Now

DOROTHY HINSHAW PATENT

Photographs by

WILLIAM MUÑOZ

DUTTON CHILDREN'S BOOKS   NEW YORK

DEDICATED TO ALL THOSE WHO ARE
EXPLORERS OF THE WONDERS OF THE EARTH

The author and photographer wish to thank Joseph Musselman, George Knapp, Ritchie Doyle, the Travelers' Rest Chapter of the Lewis and Clark Trail Heritage Foundation, and Ricardo Perez and the staff at Fort Clatsop National Memorial for their help with this book.

Background of title page: George Catlin's painting of Floyd's Grave. *National Museum of American Art, Washington, D.C./Art Resources, NY*

CIP Data is available.

Published in the United States 2002 by Dutton Children's Books,
a division of Penguin Putnam Books for Young Readers
345 Hudson Street, New York, New York 10014
www.penguinputnam.com

Designed by Richard Amari

Printed in China • First Edition
10 9 8 7 6 5 4 3 2 1
ISBN 0-525-46912-5

I've very much enjoyed writing about the Lewis and Clark Expedition and the period during which it was made. However, the discussion of some aspects of the journey has required difficult decisions. For example, the name of the Shoshone woman who accompanied Lewis and Clark has been spelled more than a dozen different ways. Most white scholars of Lewis and Clark today spell the name *Sacagawea,* as it is spelled in this book. This spelling is based on the Mandan version of her name, which means "Bird Woman." The Lemhi Shoshone Indians, however, who are descendants of her tribe, prefer the spelling *Sacajawea,* which means in their language "One Who Carries a Burden."

Because of the unreliable spelling used by the men who kept journals of the expedition and the differences in language then and now, I have changed the spelling and punctuation in the quotes from the journals that I've used to make them easier to read and understand, and have sometimes left out phrases or sentences, without indicating so.

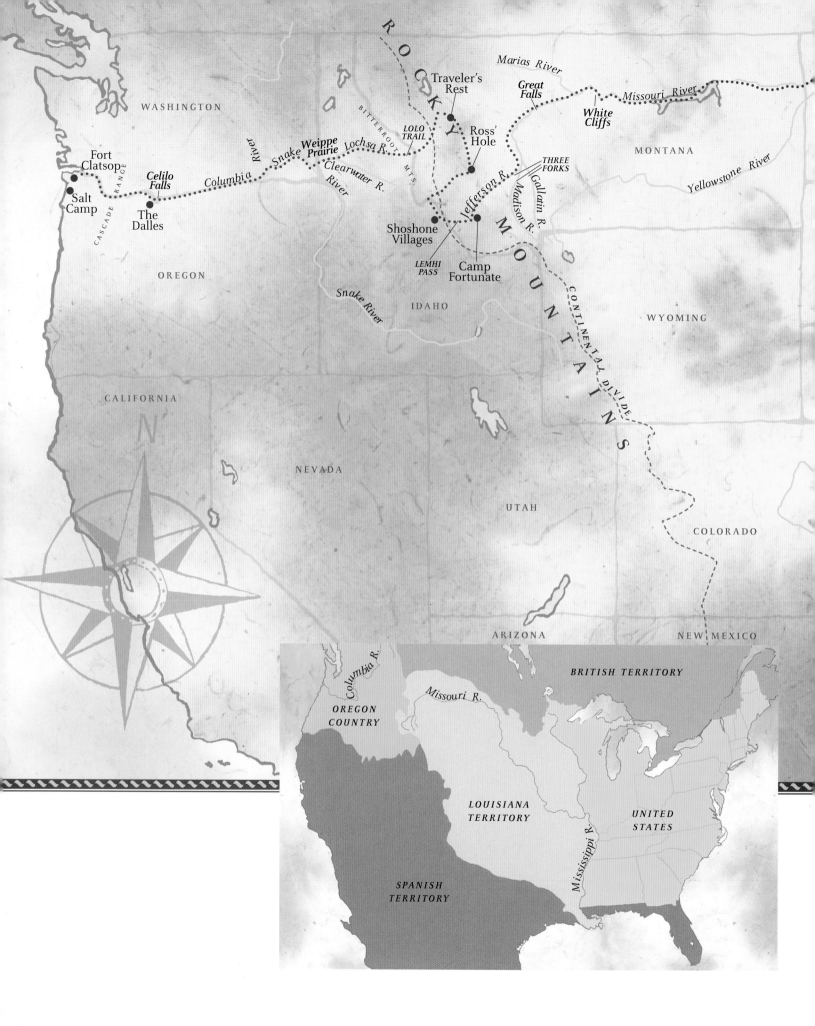

ROCKY

Marias River

Traveler's
Rest

Great
Falls

Missouri River

White
Cliffs

BITTERROOT

Ross'
Hole

MONTANA

LOLO
TRAIL

WASHINGTON

Weippe
Prairie

Lochsa R.

Snake

Columbia River

Fort
Clatsop

Celilo
Falls

Clearwater R.
River

Salt
Camp

The
Dalles

CASCADE RANGE

B
I
T
T
E
R
R
O
O
T

M
T
S
.

THREE
FORKS

Jefferson R.

Gallatin R.

Madison R.

Yellowstone River

M
O
U
N
T
A
I
N
S

Shoshone
Villages

LEMHI
PASS

Camp
Fortunate

OREGON

Snake River

IDAHO

CONTINENTAL DIVIDE

WYOMING

CALIFORNIA

N

NEVADA

UTAH

COLORADO

ARIZONA

NEW MEXICO

BRITISH TERRITORY

Columbia R.

Missouri R.

OREGON
COUNTRY

LOUISIANA
TERRITORY

UNITED
STATES

Mississippi R.

SPANISH
TERRITORY

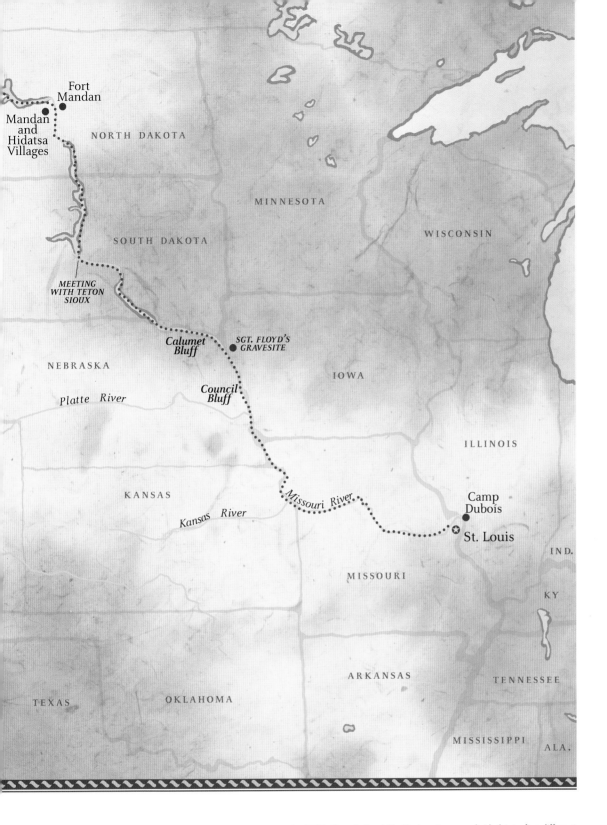

In 1803, the whole of North America was divided into five different large sections. The United States occupied the southeastern area. The British controlled the northern area as far west as the Rocky Mountain peaks. The Louisiana Territory occupied the center of the continent from the Mississippi to the Rocky Mountains. The Spanish controlled the Southwest, and the unclaimed Oregon country took up the Northwest. The route of the Lewis and Clark Expedition is also shown, with the sites mentioned in the text indicated. The Missouri River is shown as it is today, with lakes formed by modern dams.

It is two hundred years ago, and your president needs you. He has put out a call for volunteers to join a great journey of exploration. If you are selected, you will travel across unknown territory inhabited by native people who have never seen anyone other than Native Americans before. You won't know the adventures and challenges that await you. You will encounter wolves, grizzly bears, bison, and other wild creatures. With no motors to power your boats, you and your companions will have to paddle, pull, and pole strenuously upstream against a river's powerful current. Occasionally, the wind will allow you to hoist sail and rest your tired muscles.

Huge swarms of mosquitoes will dine on your blood, and you will have no repellent to fend them off. You will spend the first winter in a primitive cabin where temperatures often plunge below zero. In the spring, you will head upstream, dragging heavy canoes up steep slopes to get past towering waterfalls as the sharp spines of prickly-pear cactuses pierce your thin moccasins. You will continue through prairies and rocky canyons until you cross rugged mountains, tripping over fallen timber and struggling through deep snow. On the other side, you will descend fast-flowing rivers with churning white-water rapids until you reach your goal—the Pacific Ocean, known to seagoing fur traders. There, you will spend a second winter, this time suffering through almost constant rain and damp that rot your clothes and spoil your food.

For more than two years, your diet will be limited to a few items. You will rely mostly on game and fish that you and your companions have killed, sometimes accompanied by wild fruits and vegetables. When game is scarce, you will eat salt pork, lard, and dried corn. You

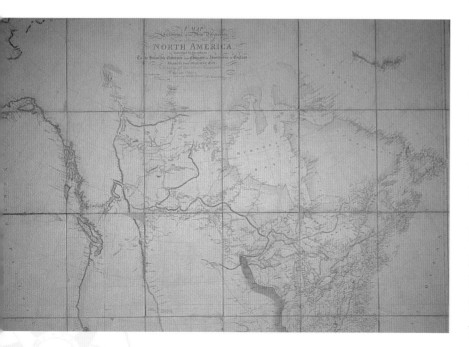

This map was made in 1802, when almost nothing was known about North America west of the Mississippi River. Jefferson wanted Meriwether Lewis and his expedition to explore the unknown areas. *Library of Congress*

will work so hard that you can easily gobble down a meal of nine pounds of meat. Many times you will go hungry. You will be completely out of touch with family and friends except for one chance to send, but not receive, letters after the first winter. Finally, you will return home, suffering many of the same hardships you had to overcome on the outward journey.

You will be rewarded by many satisfactions. You and your companions will become fast friends who share music and stories around the campfire. You will sing and dance joyfully together and revel in the excitement of new discovery. The beauty of the landscape and wildlife you encounter will astound you. Almost everything you experience will be new to you, and you will know that you are part of a great journey of discovery for your nation.

These were the experiences that awaited volunteers who joined the army expedition of Meriwether Lewis and William Clark across North America from 1804 to 1806. At that time, only about half of what is now the lower forty-eight states was known to white people. When the Lewis and Clark Expedition departed in 1804, the United States consisted of only seventeen states, all east of the Mississippi River. Major cities of today, such as Chicago and Memphis, were only frontier outposts. St. Louis, now a modern metropolis of more than 400,000 people, was a trading town of a thousand inhabitants.

Most of the route these tough adventurers traveled has changed completely during the last two hundred years, but some of it remains much as it was then. Come along now on the trail of Lewis and Clark, to compare the wilderness they explored with the America of today.

Lewis and Clark had no idea that the mountains they would encounter—the Rocky Mountains—would be this tall and rugged. The mountains they were familiar with were more like gentle, rolling hills.

The Call of the West

"The object of your mission is to explore the Missouri river. Its course &

communication with the waters of the Pacific Ocean may offer the most

direct & practicable water communication across this continent."

—*Jefferson's instructions to Lewis, June 20, 1803*

Thomas Jefferson became the third president of the United States in 1801. Even though two out of three Americans at that time lived within fifty miles of the Atlantic Ocean, Jefferson knew the nation's destiny lay to the west. Spain owned the territory called Louisiana, which extended from the Mississippi River to the Rocky Mountains. Beyond lay the unclaimed Oregon Territory. France and England were also interested in those lands, but Jefferson believed that the young United States should acquire as much of the continent as possible for its citizens. But first, the government needed to learn about the land and what it contained.

Jefferson decided to send an expedition led by his private secretary, Meriwether Lewis, to explore the uncharted West. The two men shared the same vision of the country's future. Lewis had spent much of his young life in the army in the less settled western part of what was then the United States, and Jefferson had complete faith in his abilities as a soldier and backwoodsman.

Jefferson wanted the expedition to discover a water route across the continent. In those days, rivers were vital to transportation. There were no trains, trucks, cars, or paved roads. Primitive dirt roads connected towns and cities. Getting from place to place by horse and wagon took a long time, and transporting heavy loads overland was very difficult. Boats, on the other hand, could be heavily laden and move through rivers with relative ease. When boats moved with the current, they could get from place to place with little human effort. Traveling upstream was more difficult and required manpower, but when the wind blew the right way, sails could help.

Jefferson believed boats could transport trade goods up the Missouri River to its source, wherever that might be. Then, he thought, they could be carried overland for a short distance, loaded on boats once more, and taken down the

Meriwether Lewis was chosen by Jefferson to lead the journey of exploration. After he returned, Charles Willson Peale painted his portrait, which now hangs in the Independence National Historical Park.

Columbia River to the Pacific Ocean. This would allow the United States to become a strong trading partner with faraway China.

Mapping the West was also vital to exploiting it, yet only three points could be marked on a map with confidence: St. Louis, at the junction of the Mississippi and Missouri Rivers; the Mandan Indian villages in what is now North Dakota; and the mouth of the Columbia River on the Pacific Ocean, which was visited by fur traders on ships from countries like Russia and the United States. Everything else in the vast western region remained a mystery. Jefferson instructed Lewis to record accurate celestial measurements from which latitude and longitude could be determined, especially at the mouths of rivers and other easily recognizable landmarks.

Jefferson knew that peaceful relations with the Indian tribes was vital to the interests of the United States. He also wanted to establish trade with them. He instructed Lewis to learn everything he could about Native Americans—how numerous they were, how they lived, what they hunted and ate, and so forth. The explorers took along gifts for the Indians and hoped to help the tribes make peace with one another.

As a man of great scientific curiosity, Jefferson also wanted Lewis to collect and describe specimens of minerals, plants, and animals. In 1803, the president sent Lewis to Philadelphia, where he learned from some of the most prominent scientists of the time how to skin birds and other animals, how to press plants to preserve them, and how to describe specimens scientifically.

"I will cheerfully join you and partake of the dangers, difficulties, and fatigues, and I anticipate the honors & rewards of the result of such an enterprise."

—Clark's letter of acceptance to Lewis, July 18, 1803

Lewis and Jefferson soon realized they needed a second leader, someone who would command if something happened to Lewis. Lewis knew just the man for the job—William Clark. Lewis had served under Clark for six months while on army duty from 1795 to 1796. During that time, the two men developed great mutual respect. On June 19, 1803, Lewis wrote Clark, asking him to join in the great adventure.

Today, we get quick answers to our E-mails and phone calls. But two hundred years ago, the only way to communicate over distances was by mail carried by wagon or boat. Messages took weeks or months to reach their destinations. While Lewis waited for Clark's reply, news came of an event that would make the expedition even more important. Recently, Spain had given the Louisiana Territory back to France. The French emperor, Napoleon, then sold it to the United States. This vast region stretched from the Gulf of Mexico almost to the border of modern Canada and from the Mississippi River to the Rocky Mountains. The Louisiana Purchase more than doubled the size of the United States. The explorers would be traveling through the heart of these new lands.

On July 29, 1803, Lewis received Clark's letter of acceptance. The two made a perfect team. They respected and trusted each other completely, and the personality and abilities of each complemented the other. Lewis had a scientific bent and focused much of his attention on collecting and describing plants and animals. Clark was an excellent mapmaker and a confident commander who knew how to deal with his soldiers.

The two men worked together organizing the expedition. Many young men eager for adventure, and spurred by the promise of their own land from the government upon completion of the expedition, wanted to join up. Lewis and

Lewis chose William Clark to be his partner in commanding the expedition. This portrait of Clark, also by Peale, hangs at Independence National Historical Park.

Clark carefully selected their crew, strong young men who could endure months of difficult travel and hard labor. The men came from all over the United States and from many different professions—farmer, soldier, blacksmith, hunter, carpenter, riverman, trapper. Those that weren't already in the army were sworn into it, since this was to be a military expedition.

The expedition became known as the Corps of Discovery. When it finally got under way in May 1804, it consisted of twenty-two enlisted men and three sergeants, in addition to Lewis and Clark. Also in the group was a frontiersman named George Drouillard. He had many talents, including being an excellent hunter and an expert in Indian sign language. He spoke French, English, and some Indian languages. Drouillard was officially signed on as an interpreter, but his other talents became at least as important as the expedition traveled. Clark also brought along his black slave, York. The final permanent member of the expedition was Lewis's Newfoundland dog, Seaman, whom Lewis bought in August 1803.

During the trip, other men, such as French-Canadian trappers and traders who helped row the boats or acted as interpreters, joined the Corps of Discovery temporarily until the group settled in for the winter near the Mandan Indian villages.

Lewis's dog, Seaman, was a black Newfoundland like this one. Seaman was a valuable member of the crew, helping guard the camp at night and providing companionship by day.

EQUIPMENT AND SUPPLIES

"30 Sheep skins taken off the Animal as perfectly whole as possible, without being split on the belly as usual and dressed only with lime to free them from the wool; or otherwise about the same quantity of Oil Cloth bags well painted." —From Lewis's list of equipment and supplies

One of Lewis's biggest headaches was deciding what items it was necessary to bring along. There would be no supply stations along the way, so the men of the expedition had to depend on what they already had, on what they hunted and gathered, and on what they traded for with the Indians.

Altogether, the expedition carried twelve tons of equipment and supplies. The list of items Lewis purchased ranged from ink and pencils to axes and fishhooks. Many of the things he needed are very different from what we use today. Instead of matches, he had to buy "30 steels for striking or making fire." Insect repellent was unknown, and since mosquitoes thrived along the Missouri River, mosquito netting was vitally important.

There were no man-made fabrics; everything was made from natural fibers such as cotton, wool, and linen. That meant cloth items could easily rot during the trip, and the clothing Lewis purchased was bit by bit replaced by Indian-style leather clothing. There was no such thing as plastic back then, so Lewis bought oilskin bags and metal boxes to carry the precious journals and scientific instruments. He purchased 8 x 10-foot sheets of oiled linen, which served multiple purposes. They were used as tents, sails, and covers to protect goods from rain. He needed to make sure he brought along enough wool blankets, since there were no sleeping bags.

Food was a special challenge. No one knew how long the expedition would take or how much food could be obtained by hunting and gathering. Since there was no refrigeration in those days, only food that stayed unspoiled at air temperature was brought along.

Each man in the Corps of Discovery had his own gear. Some of these copies of the items they had, such as the metal plate, are easy to identify. The square wooden plate was also used for food, which was put into the big depression, while salt went into the small one. Such plates are the origin of the phrase *three square meals a day*. On the right is old-fashioned shaving gear. In the foreground are materials needed to start a fire—a flint, striking steel, and fine fibers, called tow, that burn when a spark hits them, starting the fire.

When no wild food could be found, the men received hominy (a form of corn) and a portion of lard one day, followed by flour and salt pork the next. Lewis also had a dried mixture for "portable soup," put together for emergency rations.

Antibiotics, antihistamines, and other modern medicines had not yet been invented. Instead, Lewis brought along medicines such as Peruvian bark (for malaria), opium (for pain), and "Rush's Pills," a specially concocted medication that served many purposes.

Gifts for the Indians and items to trade with them were vitally important to the expedition. Medals with a portrait of Jefferson on one side and hands clasped in friendship on the other were given to chiefs as a sign of friendship and cooperation. The other goods—beads, twists of tobacco, metal tools—were sometimes used as gifts but were also used to trade for food and horses.

Some supplies were shared by everyone in the expedition. However, each expedition member got his own items, including a military uniform for special occasions, such as meetings with the Indians, and simple navy-blue woolen overalls for winter and white linen ones for summer. Each man also received a knapsack, a woolen blanket, a gun and a knife, a fire-starting kit, and a spoon and cup.

Of great importance were the items brought along for gifts and trade with the Indians. European Americans had many things the Indians wanted, including tobacco, strips of metal that could be turned into arrow points, metal wire with many uses, and trade beads. Blue beads were the most popular. Lewis also brought along scissors, thimbles, sewing thread, knives, combs, paint, and vermilion dye. Red was a favorite color of the native Indians to use for painting their skin.

Lewis and Clark also brought along what they called "peace medals" to give to the chiefs of the tribes. Such medals had become a traditional gift from white governments to the Indians. One side of the American medals carried a portrait of Thomas Jefferson. The other side showed two hands joined in friendship and crossed peace pipes.

Lewis and Clark each planned to keep a journal, and they encouraged other members of the expedition to do so as well. Sergeant Charles Floyd kept a journal until he became ill. Three other men, Private Joseph Whitehouse, Sergeant John Ordway, and Sergeant Patrick Gass, did so as well. All of these journals have survived to the present. The journals of another soldier disappeared.

Historian Donald Jackson wrote that Lewis and Clark were "the writingest explorers of their time. They wrote constantly and abundantly, afloat and ashore, legibly and illegibly, and always with an urgent sense of purpose." The journals were written in a total of eighteen small notebooks bound in red leather, one larger elkskin-bound notebook, other kinds of notebooks, and numerous bits and scraps of paper.

Clark kept a relatively complete record throughout the journey. Lewis, however, may have been an erratic journal keeper. Sometimes months went by without a journal entry from him. Some of Lewis's journals may have been lost. Or perhaps he suffered from a depression that kept him from writing. We will probably never know why his journals are not more complete.

Writing in those days wasn't easy. Lewis ordered a hundred quill pens for the journey. He also may have taken some brass pen tips along. A quill pen was made from the flight feathers of a goose. A penknife was used to carve the tip of the horny feather shaft into a

Lewis and Clark each started the journey with a writing desk similar to the one shown here. They wrote with quill pens, which were made from feathers. One notebook was bound in elk hide.

12

Both men wrote carefully in their journals. The left page is from one of Clark's journals, noting distance measurements that helped him make his maps. Parts of two entries by Lewis, written during the winter of 1805–1806, are on the right.

usable point. A slit leading to the tip allowed the ink to flow when the tip pressed lightly against the paper.

Lewis brought along envelopes of powdered ink. It was made from oak galls, iron sulfate, and gum arabic and was mixed with water before being used. Acid in the ink actually etched the words into the paper, creating a permanent document.

Many people have commented on the spelling the men used in the journals, especially Clark, who has been called the most creative speller of all time. For example, he spelled the word *Sioux* twenty-seven different ways! This has sometimes made understanding the journals difficult. However, Lewis and Clark departed before Noah Webster's first big dictionary was published in 1806. Spelling in those days was only beginning to be standardized, so people often spelled words the way they sounded rather than the way they were conventionally written.

These journals tell us a great deal about what North America was like before settlement by European Americans and other immigrants. Over the last two hundred years, several incomplete editions of the journals have been published. Only recently, beginning in 1986, has a complete edition, edited by Gary Moulton, been published by the University of Nebraska Press.

Winter near St. Louis

"A very smokey day. I had corn parched to make parched meal, workmen all at work preparing the boat. The Mississippi River continues to rise & discharge a great quantity of foam." —Clark's Journal, March 26, 1804

Lewis had hoped to get under way in the summer of 1803. But construction of the keelboat to be used by the expedition in Pittsburgh took much longer than expected. It was not completed until August 31. Lewis immediately gathered his crew, packed the boat, and headed down the Ohio River to the Mississippi River, then north to St. Louis. It was a rough journey, for the water level of Ohio was especially low. In the middle of October, he stopped in Clarksville, in what is now Indiana but was then the Indiana Territory, where Clark joined the voyage.

After choosing some more recruits for the expedition, Lewis and Clark left Clarksville on October 26 and arrived in the St. Louis area on November 20, 1803. Winter had already begun, and it was clear that they would have to wait out the cold weather and begin their voyage in the spring.

Lewis spoke with a Spanish government official who denied him permission to travel up the Missouri River and told him to camp on the American side of the river. Clearly, the Spanish weren't happy with the expedition, even though they knew the French would soon be taking over the vast Louisiana Territory and then transferring ownership to the United States.

The Corps of Discovery camped for the winter of 1803–1804 in a densely wooded area like this near Wood River, Illinois, across the Missouri River from St. Louis. Lewis made many trips over the Missouri to buy supplies and to recruit more men for the expedition.

The Corps of Discovery found a good campsite safely in American territory, now referred to as Camp Dubois or Wood River. During the winter, as they busied themselves with the final preparations for the expedition, the men got to know one another. Lewis and Clark made frequent trips to St. Louis to gather supplies and to finalize the selection of members of the expedition.

St. Louis had been established in 1764 to serve French fur traders. On a high

bluff overlooking the junction of the Missouri and the Mississippi Rivers, the site was an ideal center for the fur trade. Trappers brought the furs they had gathered along the lower Missouri River to sell and to trade for goods brought up the Mississippi River from New Orleans or across the continent from the East Coast.

When the Corps of Discovery arrived in the area, the town was home to French-Canadian trappers, French settlers from New Orleans, black slaves, and Indians. The people were mostly rugged folks who lived off the land.

St. Louis has been completely transformed over the last two hundred years. In 1803, there was not a single school for any age level in town. Today, the city is a thriving regional education center with five universities and twenty-six colleges. Its nickname is the "Gateway to the West," with the famous Gateway Arch welcoming visitors to explore what was once the frontier.

Today, residents of suburbs such as East St. Louis and Granite City, Illinois, commute every day to the Missouri side of the river. It's all part of the United States of America now.

George Catlin painted this picture, *St. Louis from the River Below*, in 1832–33, when the city was still just a frontier outpost. *National Museum of American Art, Washington, D.C./Art Resource, NY*

The Missouri River has shifted its course many times, and the actual site of Camp Dubois is now probably in Missouri rather than Illinois. Even so, a State Historic Site in Hartford, Illinois, honors the expedition and its campsite. St. Louis celebrates the era of the fur trade and westward expansion with museums and monuments.

Two hundred years have transformed St. Louis from a frontier village into a modern metropolis. The Gateway Arch, which welcomes travelers to the West, was completed in 1965. It is the tallest man-made monument in the world— 630 feet high.

Life on the River

"The determined and resolute character of the corps dispelled every emotion of fear, while a sense of duty, and of the honor which would attend the completion of the expedition, seemed to insure to us ample support in our future toils, suffering, and dangers."

—Patrick Gass's Journal, May 14, 1804

The main vessel used for the first part of the trip was a fifty-five-foot-long wooden keelboat. It had twenty-two oars and a mast for a sail in case of favorable winds. The expedition also had two smaller boats called pirogues, which are similar to large rowboats. One pirogue had six oars, the other seven.

On May 14, Clark and the men set off for the town of St. Charles, just up the river. There, they spent a few days waiting for Lewis, who was making final arrangements in St. Louis. Lewis joined them, and finally, on May 22, 1804, the expedition departed up the Missouri River.

Navigating the mighty Missouri challenged the crew. The current in the middle of the river was too strong to fight, so they had to progress through the shallows on either side. The unstable muddy banks sometimes collapsed, endangering both crew and boats. The men often had to push poles against the river bottom to inch the heavily laden keelboat upstream. Sometimes they attached long ropes to it and trudged along the bank or through the shallows, pulling the boat along. Always, the crew had to keep an eye out for dangerous snags. It was tough, agonizing

This reconstruction of the keelboat used by the explorers rests at the Lewis and Clark State Park in Onawa, Iowa.

work. Fourteen miles meant a very good day's progress.

As the expedition struggled up the powerful Missouri River, a daily routine emerged. The men would rise early and eat a cold breakfast so they could get under way quickly, as early as 5:00 A.M. George Drouillard and a few others headed out to hunt, while the rest of the men broke camp and loaded the boats.

Lewis and Clark agreed that at least one of them should always be on the keelboat. Clark took that role most often, using his compass to take readings as the expedition navigated the twisting and turning river. Lewis often walked the shore, taking in the lay of the land and collecting specimens of plants and animals.

They stopped for another short, cold meal at midday, then continued on

up the river. At the end of the day, they made camp on shore.

The men split up into three groups, called "messes," for dinner. One sergeant was in charge of each mess. Any meat from successful hunting was divided up, along with cornmeal, flour, or salt pork, and the cooks got busy while the rest of the men set up camp.

After dinner, the men often gathered around the campfire to exchange stories. One of them, Pierre Cruzatte, had brought along his fiddle, which turned out to be popular entertainment not only for the Corps of Discovery but for the Indians they encountered as well. When they weren't too exhausted from the exertions of the day, the men sang and danced while Cruzatte played.

While the other men slept, guards kept watch over the camp. Wild animals, severe weather, and Indians could appear during the night.

The Corps of Discovery paused to regroup at the town of St. Charles, just up the Missouri River from St. Louis. Some of its old buildings look just as they did in the early 1800s.

Working their way up the wide, often shallow Missouri was tricky for the Corps of Discovery. Today, dams regulate the river's flow, making navigation much easier.

WORKING THE WAY UPRIVER

"Two men sent out to hunt this evening brought in a buck and a poor turkey." —Clark's Journal, June 21, 1804

Ritch Doyle, who takes the role of William Clark in living history portrayals, aims a rifle like the ones used on the expedition. He steadies the weapon on a walking staff called an espontoon—a symbol of leadership. Only Lewis and Clark were allowed to carry them.

As the expedition continued up the Missouri, the men became ill with diarrhea. The leaders believed that drinking muddy water from the river caused the problem and told the men to dip their cups deeper, below the muddy surface. At this time there was no understanding of germs. Pasteur's germ theory of disease wouldn't emerge for many years, so the men of the Corps of Discovery didn't know to boil the water. Nor did they realize that meat several days old could cause sickness. People in those days also had little understanding of nutrition. They didn't realize that a diet of meat, lard, flour, and cornmeal, with almost no fruits or vegetables, could be a cause of the painful boils the men developed on their skin.

Fresh meat, however, made for much better eating than salt pork, and guns were necessary for hunting. Lewis had ordered fifteen of the most modern guns available, Harper's Ferry Model 1803 flintlock rifles. They were so new that his crew was the first to obtain them. These rifles were very accurate for the time. A hunter could strike an elk at a hundred and fifty yards. By today's standards, the rifles were primitive, but compared to the more common musket, they were a big advance. The inside of a musket barrel is smooth, while that of a rifle is "rifled," meaning it has spiral grooves. The grooves force the bullet to spin as it goes through the barrel and out, which gives it a more accurate flight toward the target.

Now we have guns that can fire a thousand bullets a minute. Back then, the rifle had to be reloaded before each shot. The bullet was a handmade lead sphere. The very best soldiers took thirty seconds to load a gun.

The men had to make their own bullets. A pistol typical of their time is shown here, along with the materials necessary for making bullets. On the right is a replica of the lead canisters Lewis designed to keep gunpowder dry.

To make bullets, the lead was melted in a small pot. The hot lead was carefully ladled into a mold. After the lead hardened, the handles of the mold were opened and the ball rolled out. The bits of extra lead were clipped off, and the surface was smoothed.

The first step in loading the rifle was pouring a measured amount of gunpowder into the barrel. Next, the lead ball, topped by a small patch of cloth, was jammed in, using the ramrod stored below the barrel. Then a small amount of gunpowder was placed on the pan above the trigger. The soldier then cocked the gun, aimed, and fired. When the trigger was pulled, the flint hammer struck a piece of steel right above the pan, showering sparks down into the pan. A small hole in the barrel carried the spark to the gunpowder in the barrel, igniting it. The explosion of the powder in the barrel sent the ball flying out toward the target.

Lewis devised a clever way of transporting the lead and powder. Most of the travel would be by water, and the powder had to be kept dry. Lewis had fifty-two lead canisters made, each containing eight pounds of lead. Each canister was filled with four pounds of powder, just the amount needed to fire the balls made from the lead in one canister. The tops of the canisters were sealed with wax to keep the powder dry.

Entering Indian Country

"Children we have been sent by the great Chief of the Seventeen great nations [states] of America to inform you that all who live in this area are bound to obey the commands of their great Chief the President who is now your only great father."

—Clark quoting Lewis's speech to the Indians

The Corps of Discovery arrived at the mouth of the Kansas River on June 26, 1804. They'd been under way for more than a month and needed a break. They stayed there for four days, hunting deer, resting, drying out their goods.

Jefferson had instructed Lewis to determine the exact location of important points like this so they could be located by other travelers, so Lewis also took careful measurements with his sextant. Today, we have satellites that can pinpoint any spot on the earth's surface accurately. But back then, the sextant was a modern tool that measured the angles between the stars, sun, and moon. These measurements make it possible to determine the latitude and longitude of a place. Lewis and Clark themselves could use the numbers to ascertain latitude, but determining longitude was much more complicated and had to be done later by experts.

Using a sextant is difficult, and Lewis had been taught how to use one while he was in Pennsylvania. Despite all the time and effort Lewis and sometimes Clark put into taking these measurements, little use was made of them later.

As the Corps of Discovery continued upriver that spring, the men's spirits rose. The lush prairie bloomed, birds sang, and delicious wild fruits hung from the bushes. They passed the mouth of the Platte River in present-day Nebraska on July 21, 1804. Fifty years later, pioneers bound for California, Oregon, and Utah would follow the Platte westward in their covered wagons.

A sextant was used to make measurements that helped determine longitude and latitude.

The expedition entered the tallgrass prairie, covered with wildflowers as well as grass. Today more than 98 percent of the grass has been plowed to make room for crops like corn and for cities and towns.

Before Europeans came to North America, the continent was inhabited by dozens and dozens of Indian tribes, each with its own culture and homeland. Soon after Europeans arrived, the Indians' way of life began to disappear. Diseases brought by the new settlers killed large numbers of Indians. Whites and Indians also fought over land, and the whites, with their superior weapons, usually won.

By 1804, many of the tribes east of the Mississippi had been eliminated, but many tribes still inhabited the West. While war and disease brought by white men had already weakened many western tribes, Indian culture was still strong. Lewis and Clark were eager to meet with the Indians and let them know their lands were now under American rule and that the Americans wanted peaceful relations with them.

Meeting the Indians proved difficult at first, however, as most of them were out on the plains hunting buffalo. Finally, on August 3, 1804, Lewis and Clark held their first Indian council with the Oto and Missouri, who had brought along a French trader as a translator. These tribes farmed as well as hunted, so they had semipermanent settlements near the river. Lewis gave a long speech telling the Indians that their new white father (President Jefferson) wanted peace among the tribes.

At the base of Council Bluff in Nebraska, Lewis and Clark had their first Indian council when they met with the Oto and Missouri. Since then, the Missouri River has changed course to the east, so the site is now some distance from the river.

After Lewis finished talking, the Indians spoke, acknowledging his words and asking for gunpowder and whiskey in addition to the medals, combs, and other gifts they were given. Lewis obliged. Two important chiefs were not at the meeting, so it was difficult for the Americans to draw any certain conclusions, but their first Indian encounter seemed to have gone well.

Life and Death Along the River

SGT. FLOYD'S GRAVESITE

NEBRASKA

IOWA

Platte River

Council Bluff

Missouri River

KANSAS

"Sergeant Floyd died, notwithstanding every possible effort to save his life. We interred his remains in the most decent manner our circumstances would admit. We proceeded to a small river and our commanding officers gave it the name of Floyd's River to perpetuate the memory of the first man who had fallen in this important expedition…"

—Patrick Gass's Journal, August 20, 1804

On August 8, 1804, the men saw a mysterious white blanket covering the river as far as they could see upstream. As they came nearer, they realized the blanket was made up of millions of feathers. Where had they come from?

Not far upriver, the expedition came upon an island densely packed with white pelicans. The birds were gathered together while they molted, shedding their old feathers and growing new ones. It was these molted feathers that had formed the three-mile-long blanket. Lewis wanted to shoot a specimen, but dense clouds of mosquitoes made aiming his rifle impossible. The birds were so tightly packed, however, that a random shot killed one. Even though much of the land along the lower Missouri River today is prone to flooding and therefore sparsely populated, white pelicans have become a rare sight in the area.

On August 20, 1804, Sergeant Charles Floyd became the only casualty of the entire trip and the first United States soldier to die west of the Mississippi River. For several days, he had been in agony, probably from an infected appendix that had ruptured. Even today, when a ruptured appendix is a painful but treatable problem, such an illness could be fatal in the wilderness. Surgery repairs the physical damage, and antibiotics kill the infection that spreads through the body when the appendix bursts.

Sergeant Floyd was buried on a hill near the river. In 1857, his remains were moved to the town of Sioux City, Iowa, because the river was eating away the hill. Today, a monument there honors him.

After Floyd's funeral, the explorers continued up the river, marveling at the abundance of game—beaver, deer, elk, and finally buffalo. On August 23, one of

White pelicans are no longer as abundant as they were at the time of Lewis and Clark, but they still gather in places along the Missouri River.

George Catlin painted Floyd's Grave in 1832, to commemorate the burial of Sergeant Floyd on a hilltop overlooking the Missouri River. *National Museum of American Art, Washington, D.C./Art Resource, NY*

the men killed a buffalo, and they got their first taste of this great beast.

The buffalo was the basis of the Plains Indian cultures. The Indians used every part of the animal—for food, tools, clothing, and tepee construction. In those days, the buffalo moved across the plains in huge herds that sometimes took days to pass by. Later in the 1800s, however, commercial hunters slaughtered all the buffalo they could find, almost wiping them out.

In the late 1800s and early 1900s, buffalo hunting was banned. By 1900, only twenty wild buffalo survived in the United States, living in the backcountry of Yellowstone National Park. A few hundred also remained in private herds, and about two hundred and fifty lived in Canada. Efforts began to rescue the buffalo from extinction. Herds were established on refuges in Oklahoma and Montana, and recovery of the animal was under way. Today, buffalo live in several national parks and preserves. Ranchers and Indian tribes also maintain herds of these powerful, hardy animals, and buffalo meat is increasing in popularity. Still, where once millions of these magnificent animals roamed the prairies, now perhaps only a hundred thousand survive.

Within the city limits of Sioux City, Iowa, this hundred-foot-tall monument to Floyd stands on top of his burial site.

Buffalo once roamed the prairies in gigantic herds that helped feed the Lewis and Clark Expedition.

MEETING THE SIOUX

"At 9 o'clock we made preparations to sail; some of the chiefs were on board,

and concluded to go some distance with us. When we went to shove off,

some of the Indians took hold of the rope and would not let go.

This conduct had like to be attended with bad consequences, as Captain

Lewis was near giving orders to cut the rope and to fire on them."

—Patrick Gass's Journal, September 28, 1804

Lewis and Clark knew how important and potentially dangerous meeting the Sioux would be. This largest of Indian tribes controlled trade on the Missouri River. The Sioux had turned back the boats of American traders from St. Louis before. Lewis wanted to convince them to cooperate with the new government in Washington and allow open passage for Americans along the river.

In late August 1804, the expedition encountered an encampment of the Yankton branch of the Sioux tribe. On the morning of August 30, the whites and Indians held a council at Calumet Bluff. Lewis spoke of the president's desires, and a French-Canadian trader named Pierre Dorion, who was married to a Yankton Sioux woman, translated. Lewis gave medals to each of the five chiefs who had come. As with other tribes, he chose one chief—in this case a man named Weuche (wee-OO-chay)—as the head chief and presented him with a military uniform and an American flag.

During the Corps of Discovery's visit with the Teton Sioux, the tribe held a scalp dance celebrating a victory over the Omahas. Clark described the scene: "A large fire made in the center, about 10 musicians playing on tambourines made of hoops & skin stretched.... Men began to sing and beat on the tambourine, the women came forward highly decorated in their way, with the scalps and trophies of war of their fathers, husbands, brothers, or near connection and proceeded to dance the war dance." Artist George Catlin expresses the mood in this painting from 1835–1837. *National Museum of American Art, Washington, D.C./Art Resource, NY*

A visitors' center above Gavins Point Dam near Yankton, South Dakota, offers tourists information about the Calumet Bluff council with the Yankton Sioux.

That evening, the Indians and the Americans entertained one another with music and dancing. The next morning, the chiefs came again to talk to the whites. Like the Otos and Missouris, the Yankton Sioux were most concerned about reliable trade. Weuche agreed to go to Washington to meet the president in the spring as long as Mr. Dorion went along. The Yankton warned Lewis and Clark that their upriver relatives, the Teton Sioux, would be harder to deal with. After presenting the chiefs with tobacco, the explorers left. Dorion stayed behind with his wife's people.

On September 23, they encountered the Teton Sioux near present-day Pierre, South Dakota, and on the twenty-forth, the two groups held a council. Unfortunately, Pierre Cruzatte, the expedition's French-Canadian translator, knew only a few words of the Teton language, which made communication difficult. The Americans remained near the Sioux camp until September 28. During that time, the two groups struggled to influence and intimidate each other. Twice, both sides were poised for battle. The Teton Sioux were determined to retain control of trade along the river, and the Americans were just as determined to convince the Indians to become part of an American trading system and to let the expedition continue up the Missouri. When the Corps of Discovery finally left, neither side had given in, and the Teton Sioux continued their harassment of American traders for years to come.

SETTLING ON A WINTER HOME

"This Mandan village contains houses in a kind of picket work.
The houses are round and very large, containing several families,
as also their horses which are tied on one side of the entrance. I walked
up and smoked a pipe with the chiefs of the village. They were anxious
that I would stay and eat with them." —Clark's Journal, October 27, 1804

Through the fall of 1804 travel went smoothly for the Corps of Discovery. The men had mastered the boats, the weather remained beautiful, and migrating game was abundant. In early September, the Corps of Discovery had entered a new kind of territory, the mixed-grass prairie, where plentiful animals provided abundant game. The men rarely had to eat hominy and lard or salt pork and flour. Every man wolfed down several pounds of fresh meat each day, accompanied by cornmeal and wild fruit. When the wind came from the right direction, the travelers could spread sails to help speed the boats upriver. Best of all, perhaps, nighttime frosts killed off the swarms of mosquitoes that had plagued them all summer.

Today, the wild prairie has been replaced by vast fields of wheat, oats, and other grains. Near Pierre, the capital of South Dakota, Oahe Dam on the Missouri holds back a large reservoir and provides flood control and power as well as irrigation water for farmers.

As October waned, the expedition entered what is now North Dakota. On October 24, 1804, Lewis and Clark met with their first Mandan people. This tribe

While the tallgrass prairie has been plowed under to grow corn, the mixed-grass prairie has been replaced by crops such as wheat and barley.

hunted and farmed, like the Otos and Missouris. Their villages formed the center for trade in the Northern Plains. In late summer and early fall, whites and Indians alike came from hundreds of miles around to trade horses, clothing, guns, corn, tobacco, and other products of both Indian and white culture.

Just forty years earlier, the Mandans had inhabited nine villages lower down on the Missouri River. But the combination of deadly smallpox brought to them by white men and attacks by the Sioux had reduced their numbers dramatically. When the Corps of Discovery arrived, the Mandan lived in just two villages about three miles apart. Nearby, to the north, lay three villages of another tribe, the much-reduced Hidatsas. These villages, near present-day Bismarck, North Dakota, formed the last spot on the Missouri River that could be accurately located on maps.

This reconstruction of Fort Mandan shows the rough wooden walls and tall stockade fence that provided security for the Corps during the winter of 1804–1805.

The Mandans and Hidatsas proved friendly to the Americans and were happy the Corps would spend the winter nearby. At the beginning of November 1804, the Americans settled on a site on the east side of the Missouri, across the river from the nearest Mandan village. Clark estimated that they had traveled 1,609 miles along the tortuous, twisting Missouri River over the past five and a half months.

The Americans had to build a fort. They cut down trees, trimmed them, and constructed two rows of buildings at right angles to each other. The highest walls, which faced the outside, reached eighteen feet, forming two of the outer walls of the fort. The soldiers also built a tall picket fence on the other two sides to enclose the yard. Lewis and Clark wanted a secure fort, safe from Indian attack. The Mandans were friendly, but that could change, and the Sioux always posed a threat.

While the soldiers were building the fort, Lewis and Clark signed on a French-Canadian fur trader named Toussaint Charbonneau, who lived with the Hidatsa. Charbonneau agreed to bring along one of his two Shoshone Indian wives, Sacagawea. The Shoshone lived on the edge of the Rocky Mountains, and Lewis and Clark were counting on getting horses from them to cross the mountains. In addition to being a translator, Sacagawea turned out to be an asset to the expedition in many ways.

Getting Through the Winter

"This morning was fair tho cold, thermometer at 14 below zero. A little after dark this evening Capt. Clark arrived with the hunting party. Since they set out they have killed forty deer, three buffalo bulls, & sixteen elk, most of them were so meager that they were unfit for use. The wolves, which are here extremely numerous, helped themselves to a considerable proportion of the hunt. If an animal is killed and lies only one night exposed to the wolves, it is almost invariably devoured by them."

—Lewis's Journal, February 12, 1805

The Fort Mandan winter was especially cold and brutal, with temperatures often falling below zero. The cold didn't stop the military routine, however, with regular drills, weapons inspections, and sentry duties. Sometimes the temperatures dropped so low that the sentries changed every half hour to avoid frostbite.

The men had to endure the cold to hunt, often along with the Indians. Toward the end of the winter, many of the animals they shot were in such poor condition—"meager," the men said—that the meat wasn't worth taking to camp. Luckily for the Corps of Discovery, the Indians had plenty of stored corn, which they were happy to trade for American goods or blacksmith services. Private John Shields was an accomplished blacksmith and used the forge he set up to repair cooking pots and to make battle-axes.

The soldiers and the Indians also liked being together. They visited back and

Sturdy earth lodges like this one, buried beneath snow, kept the Mandan Indians comfortable year round. They were easier to keep warm than the soldiers' wooden fort.

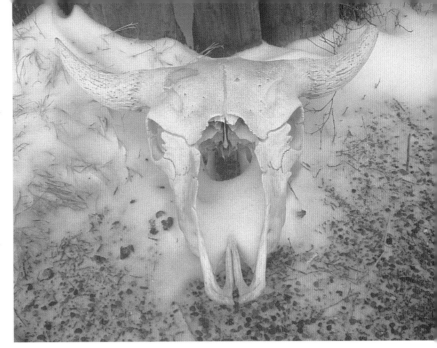

forth from the fort to the villages and enjoyed each other's music and dancing. Each group invited the other to share in their special celebrations.

As spring began, the Corps prepared for departure. They had to get two groups ready. A few men would go back down the Missouri, taking plant and animal specimens as well as reports with them. In these days of instant communication, it's hard to believe that Lewis and Clark had had no contact with Jefferson since setting out the previous May. Lewis had so much to tell the president, and he knew this would almost certainly be his last chance to communicate until the Corps of Discovery returned many months later.

During the long winter, Lewis wrote page after page about the habits and culture of the Indian tribes he had encountered. All this information had to be copied to send to Jefferson, who wanted to learn everything he could about the tribes he would soon be dealing with in earnest.

Lewis and Clark had also talked extensively with the Indians about what lay to the west, and that information needed to be sent to Jefferson as well. Lewis's report focused on the rivers, since they were vital to transportation. Clark prepared a map of the new United States territory west of the Missouri River. The men included only information they themselves had discovered or descriptions that different Indians agreed upon. If the Corps of Discovery should fail and never return, at least Jefferson would have that much information about the little-known Louisiana Territory.

The specimens they sent included minerals, animal skins and bones, and dried plants, as well as a few live animals—four magpies, a prairie dog, and a prairie grouse hen. On April 7, 1805, the shipment to Jefferson headed downriver in the expedition's keelboat under the command of Captain Warfington. Lewis and Clark took their two pirogues and six canoes on the upstream journey into unknown territory. They brought along a tepee for themselves, George Drouillard, Charbonneau, and Sacagawea and her young baby, Jean Baptiste, born during the winter. Clark affectionately nicknamed him "Pomp."

Sometimes during the harsh winter, the Indians and whites managed to hunt buffalo successfully. But the supply of meat was unreliable, and stored corn became vital to survival.

WHERE THE YELLOWSTONE MEETS THE MISSOURI

"I ascended to the top of the cut bluff this morning, from whence I had a most delightful view of the country, the whole of which, except the valley formed by the Missouri, is void of timber or underbrush, exposing to the first glance of the spectator immense herds of buffalo, elk, deer, and antelopes feeding in one common and boundless pasture...."

—Lewis's Journal, April 17, 1805

On April 15, 1805, the explorers passed the farthest point previously reached by fur trappers. Now they entered territory completely new to European Americans. The nights were frosty and the days pleasant. At first, the wind served as an ally, filling the sails of the boats and pushing them upriver. But after a few days, it became so strong that they had difficulty traveling at all.

This area, called the northern plains, teemed with buffalo, deer, elk, and pronghorn. The hunters brought in abundant game, so everyone had plenty to eat. Lewis and Clark commented on the abundance of game and the beauty of the landscape over and over again in their journals as they traveled through what we now call the short-grass prairie.

Lake Sakakawea, retained by the Garrison Dam in North Dakota, now holds a large stretch of the Missouri River. The Fort Berthold Indian Reservation, set aside for the Mandan, Hidatsa, and Arikara nations, occupies much of the area around this large lake.

The land around the junction of the Yellowstone and Missouri Rivers teemed with game in 1805. Lewis wrote: "The whole face of the country was covered with herds of buffalo, elk, & antelopes." Today, the once abundant wildlife has disappeared.

Today, this region along the western edge of North Dakota and eastern Montana is cattle country. Few people live there, but most of the wild grasses and flowers have been replaced by grass cattle prefer. The abundant wildlife is almost gone, although some pronghorn and mule deer survive. However, bison, elk, and bighorn sheep have been returned to two pieces of land that total 70,448 acres, called Theodore Roosevelt National Park. South of the Missouri River in western North Dakota, oil and natural-gas wells dot the landscape.

On April 25, Lewis and four men hiked along the Missouri's southern shore to the mouth of the Yellowstone River. The Hidatsa, whose war parties had traveled all the way to the base of the Rocky Mountains, told Lewis the Yellowstone was the largest of all the rivers that flowed into the Missouri from the west. Reaching this spot had become a major goal of the expedition, so Lewis took the time to make careful measurements with his sextant. Clark measured the width of both rivers where they joined. Both men realized the site would be a good place to build a fort. Lewis commented in his journal about the abundant limestone, which would make an excellent building material. Clark pointed out a high spot with a commanding view of the surrounding countryside. Twenty-four years later, a trading post called Fort Union was built on the north shore. It is now a National Historic Site.

THE PUZZLE OF THE MARIAS RIVER

"The bluffs of the river rise to the height of from 2 to 200 feet and in most places nearly perpendicular. The water in the course of time had trickled down the soft sand cliffs and worn it into a thousand grotesque figures of lofty freestone buildings, having their parapets well stocked with statuary; columns of various sculpture are also seen. In other places we see the remains or ruins of elegant buildings."

—Lewis's Journal, May 31, 1805

On April 28, 1805, the expedition left the mouth of the Yellowstone River and continued up the Missouri with the wind in its sails. As they worked their way up the river, the explorers encountered difficulties ranging from aggressive grizzly bears they had to shoot to wild gusts of wind that almost upset one of the pirogues. As May drew to a close, they entered one of the most dramatically beautiful stretches of the Missouri River. Here, barren cliffs jut up from the shore, first golden-brown sandstone and later white. Today, this stretch is preserved as the Upper Missouri National Wild and Scenic River and offers canoeists and rafters a glimpse of the untouched country encountered by the Corps of Discovery.

To Lewis and Clark, however, the land was like a barren desert. One of their main concerns was determining the value of the land they passed through for farming by American settlers, and this steep, rocky region looked very unpromising.

On May 26, Lewis climbed the steep bluffs and looked to the west. Far in the distance, he could see mountains. "While I viewed these mountains I felt a secret pleasure in finding myself so near the head of the heretofore conceived boundless Missouri," he wrote.

On June 3, the explorers came upon an unexpected difficulty, a fork in the river the Indians hadn't told them about. Lewis had questioned the Mandan and Hidatsa Indians over and over about what they knew of the lands to the west. How could they have missed telling him about this important river, which Lewis named Maria's River, after his cousin Maria

The white cliffs of the Missouri River, east of the Marias River, are as spectacular today as they were in Lewis and Clark's time.

Near its junction with the Marias, the Missouri River probably looks today much as it did in 1805 when the Corps of Discovery worried over which river to take.

Wood? The Indians traveled on horses across the land, not in boats on the rivers. The Missouri loops to the north, where Maria's River, now called the Marias, joins it. Traveling on land, Indians would have worked their way more directly across the plains, so they probably didn't even know about the other river.

Which branch should the Corps of Discovery take? The men all thought the north (right-hand) fork was the Missouri. Its water was brownish, like that of the Missouri. Lewis reasoned, however, that the muddiness of the north fork meant it traveled many miles through the plains, picking up soil on its way. The clearness of the south fork, he felt, meant that it came right down from the mountains. Clark agreed.

After scouting both forks, Lewis and Clark decided to follow their instincts and proceed up the south fork. The men showed their faith in their leaders by accepting the choice without complaint. Everyone knew how important this decision was—a wrong decision could mean wasting critical time, likely resulting in failure of the expedition.

Before continuing their journey, they hid one of their pirogues and many supplies at the rivers' junction. Such a place is called a cache (pronounced "cash"). At this place, Lewis could see that they had to lighten their load for the steep ascent into the mountains. Several more times along the way, the men of the expedition "cached" items they wouldn't need until the return trip.

A Plains Indian–style tepee stands along the Upper Missouri National Wild and Scenic River.

Caching could be risky. When Lewis opened the cache at the Great Falls on his return, in July 1806, he found it had flooded, ruining all his plant specimens and some bearskins.

THE GREAT FALLS

"Projecting rocks below receive the water in its passage down and break it into perfect white foam which assumes a thousand forms in a moment, sometimes flying up in jets of sparkling foam to the height of fifteen or twenty feet." —Lewis's Journal, June 13, 1805

The Hidatsa had told the explorers about a giant waterfall on the Missouri. If the explorers came to the falls, they would know they'd taken the right fork in the river. The Hidatsa had said there was just a single waterfall, so Lewis thought they could get around it in half a day.

On June 13, 1805, Lewis hiked ahead on land, looking for the waterfall. When he climbed a hill to overlook plains that teemed with buffalo, a welcome sound reached his ears—the roar of water falling from a great height. He wrote: "…advancing a little further I saw the spray arise above the plain like a column of smoke. It soon began to make a roaring too tremendous to be mistaken for any cause short of the great falls of the Missouri."

The magnificence of the falls overwhelmed Lewis. He felt his words totally inadequate to the task of describing its power and beauty. He continued up the river, expecting to find calm water above the falls. Instead, the rapids went on for five miles. Even worse, he then came across a second falls, then a third, a fourth, and a fifth!

The magnificent Great Falls of the Missouri River before they were dammed.

Getting around the falls became a nightmare. The men cached the second pirogue and other items, then made crude wagons from a cottonwood tree. They cut up the mast of the pirogue to make axles for the wagons. As they pushed and pulled the wagons over the rough ground, thick clouds of mosquitoes and hail as big as apples plagued them, along with the hot sun and the sharp spines of the prickly-pear cactus that seemed to blanket the ground.

Ryan Dam now holds back the Missouri where once the Great Falls roared. A remnant of the falls appears just below the dam.

Giant Springs, which flows into the Missouri River near Great Falls, is one of the largest freshwater springs in the world, with a daily flow of 388.8 million gallons. Summer or winter, the temperature of the water stays at fifty-four degrees.

Today, the town of Great Falls, Montana, sits on the banks of the Missouri. A series of dams now controls the once mighty river and provides electrical power for the inhabitants and irrigation water for farmers. Only remnants of the falls and rapids remain.

The land around Great Falls is now used for growing wheat. Wheat fields stretch from the edge of town far beyond the horizon. Great Falls is also the home of the Lewis and Clark National Historical Trail Interpretive Center, a museum that traces the route of the explorers and the lives of the Indian tribes they encountered.

Finally, a month after Lewis reached the Great Falls, the Corps of Discovery was once again under way up the Missouri, now traveling in eight new dugout canoes the men had made. As they paddled into the mountains, it became more and more difficult to travel up the faster flowing, shallower river. Lewis and Clark were now in search of Sacagawea's people, the Shoshone.

As the expedition neared the land of the Shoshone, Sacagawea was able to recognize landmarks. The captains took turns walking on land, looking for signs of the Indians. On July 25, 1805, a group led by Clark arrived at the origin of the Missouri River, called Three Forks. In his journal entry for July 27, Lewis names the rivers—the southeast fork became Gallitin's River, "in honor of Albert Gallitin Secretary of the Treasury." "The Middle fork we called Maddison's River in honor of James Maddison the Secretary of State." The southwest fork became Jefferson's River, in honor of the president. While many of the names Lewis and Clark gave to rivers were later changed, these three names remain to this day, although the spelling of Gallatin and Madison has been corrected.

Finding the Shoshone

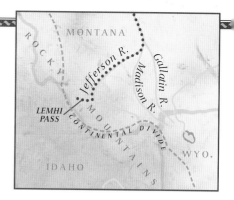

"The road took us to the most distant fountain of the waters of the Mighty Missouri in search of which we have spent so many toilsome days and restless nights. Thus far I had accomplished one of those great objects on which my mind has been unalterably fixed for many years."

—Lewis's Journal, August 12, 1805

When Sacagawea spotted Beaverhead Rock, she told Lewis and Clark that "the summer retreat of her nation" was not far away.

As they searched for the Shoshone, Lewis and Clark knew they were on the right track because Sacagawea recognized another landmark, a hill by the river that looked like a beaver's head. Still, the Indians were hard to find. While Clark and most of the expedition, including Sacagawea, struggled up ever-narrower waterways, Lewis took along two men to look for the Shoshone on land. On the morning of August 12, 1805, Lewis and his men climbed up an old Indian road. The road led to a spring that fed a small creek. Here, water that would become the great Missouri River began its course toward the Atlantic Ocean. Lewis drank from the creek triumphantly.

Lewis wrote "after refreshing ourselves we proceeded on to the top of the dividing ridge from which I discovered immense ranges of high mountains still to the west of us with their tops partially covered with snow." He stood at Lemhi Pass, part of the Continental Divide, a great, jagged ridge that divides waters flowing toward the Atlantic Ocean from those that end up in the Pacific Ocean. At the time, the term *Continental Divide* hadn't been coined yet, but Lewis realized that on the other side he would find waters that flowed into the Columbia. After crossing the ridge and climbing down the other side, the men found, as Lewis wrote, "a handsome bold running creek of cold clear water. Here I first tasted the water of the great Columbia River."

For the first time, American citizens had gazed upon the rugged expanse of the Rocky Mountains and crossed the Continental Divide. In this area, the Rockies are about two hundred and fifty miles wide,

The men searched through these hills, which have changed very little in two hundred years, looking for the Shoshone.

and Lewis was only about halfway across. Jefferson's dream of an easy portage from the Missouri River system across the mountains to the Columbia was clearly dashed.

On August 13, they finally made contact with a band of Lemhi Shoshone. After Lewis gave them a few presents, an old woman, a little girl, and a teenage girl were convinced to lead them to the tribe. As the group walked toward the encampment, a band of sixty armed warriors galloped up to meet them. Lewis put down his rifle, told his men to stay put, and walked toward the war party carrying only an American flag.

Lewis's brave act calmed the Shoshone, and the men sat down together and smoked the peace pipe. Lewis gave out gifts and presented a flag to the main chief, named Cameahwait (Cam-EE-ah-wait). The Shoshone escorted the strangers to their camp, where they smoked together once again. Curious women and children marveled at these strange men with skin as "pale as ashes." They had never seen white men before.

Lewis's simple gifts charmed the Indians, who passed on this lovely description of the mirrors they were given: "things like solid water, which were sometimes brilliant as the sun, and which sometimes showed us our faces."

Lewis and Privates John Shields and Hugh McNeal strode up the slope leading to the Continental Divide. Lewis wrote in his journal, "McNeal exultingly stood with a foot on each side of this little rivulet and thanked his god that he has lived to bestride the mighty & heretofore deemed endless Missouri."

After crossing the Continental Divide and walking down the other side, Lewis drank from this spring, whose waters flow down to the Columbia and end up in the Pacific Ocean. The Continental Divide marked the border of the Louisiana Territory. Here, Lewis and his men were no longer on land claimed by the United States.

AMONG THE SHOSHONE

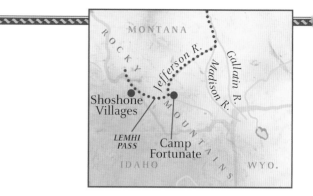

"Sacagawea was sent for; she came into the tent, sat down, and was beginning to interpret, when in the person of Cameahwait she recognized her brother: she instantly jumped up, and ran and embraced him, throwing over him her blanket and weeping profusely."

—Nicholas Biddle's version of the journals, August 17, 1805

Despite their warm greetings, the Shoshone weren't sure about these strangers. Were they allies of their enemies, the Blackfeet? Lewis did his best to reassure them, telling them that a woman from their tribe was part of his group.

Only after Clark's group finally joined them did the suspicion disappear. Cameahwait, who must have been just as relieved as Lewis to meet peaceably, welcomed Clark with hugs and decorated his hair with precious shells from the faraway Pacific Ocean. Once again, the peace pipe was smoked.

Sacagawea was delighted to be with her people once more. She soon recognized one of the women as a friend who had also been kidnapped by the Hidatsa but who had managed to escape. The two young women hugged and talked excitedly together.

The white men set up camp by the Beaverhead River. In the afternoon, the whites and the Indians held a conference under a canopy formed by one of the boat sails. Lewis asked Sacagawea to join them and interpret. As she began to translate, she recognized that Cameahwait was her brother! She ran to him, hugging him and crying with joy.

The site of Camp Fortunate, where the Corps of Discovery met with the Shoshone, is now underwater, covered by Clark Canyon Reservoir. Interstate Highway 15 runs nearby.

Sacagawea had trouble controlling her emotions during the meeting. Communicating took time, for the translation process was complicated. Cameahwait spoke to his sister in Shoshone. She related his words in Hidatsa to Charbonneau, who translated them into French. Finally, Private Labiche, a French-Canadian member of the Corps, related the information to the Americans in English.

The Corps named the campsite Camp Fortunate because of their good luck with the Shoshone. The men busied themselves there with preparations for crossing the Rockies, aided by the Shoshone. Boxes and canoe-paddle blades were broken up and rebuilt into pack saddles for the horses. Items were selected for another cache in order to lighten the load. An Indian whom Lewis and Clark called "Old Toby" agreed to guide the Corps of Discovery across the mountains.

In his painting of the meeting between the Corps of Discovery and the Shoshone, the artist J. K. Ralston tried to fit in everything about the visit with the Indians—warriors on horseback, Indians examining York, Sacagawea and her baby Pomp, and horses with Western-style saddles. *National Park Service*

Without Sacagawea's help, the Corps of Discovery almost certainly would have failed before crossing the Rocky Mountains. She helped them locate the land of her people, and her presence convinced the Shoshone that the white men were not enemies. She also made conversation between the two groups possible. A new visitors' center near Lemhi Pass honors Sacagawea and her contributions to the expedition.

Today, the site of Camp Fortunate lies under the waters of Clark Canyon Reservoir, built in 1963 to store water for farmers to irrigate their crops. Interstate Highway 15 runs alongside the reservoir, south of Dillon, Montana.

On August 30, 1805, the Corps of Discovery finally continued on its way. The Shoshone had supplied them with twenty-nine horses in return for trade goods and clothing. The route was extremely rugged. As Clark wrote on September 3, "We passed over immense hills and some of the worst road that ever horses passed. Our horses frequently fell." The expedition's last thermometer broke during one of these accidents.

Their luck seemed to have turned bad. That day, it snowed. They had to eat the last of their salt pork, for no game could be found. The country through which they passed was so wild and confusing that they were unable to describe it well. No one today is sure just where they crossed these mountains, but it must have been near modern Lost Trail Pass. Most of this area is still wild, without roads or human inhabitants. U.S. Highway 93, however, passes through the area, and Lost Trail Pass is now the site of a ski area.

THE BITTERROOT VALLEY

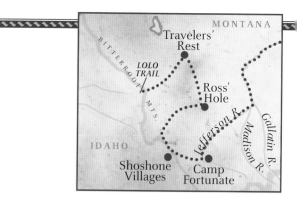

"The road through this hilly country is very bad, passing over hills &
through steep hollows, over falling timber &c &c Continued on &
passed some most intolerable road on the sides of the steep stony
mountains, which might be avoided by keeping up the creek,
which is thickly covered with undergrowth & falling timber."

—Clark's Journal, September 12, 1805

Tired and sore, the explorers finally descended the western side of the Continental Divide, ending up near the headwaters of the Bitterroot River. There they encountered a band of about four hundred Salish Indians on September 4, 1805.

The Salish were unfamiliar with whites and had never seen such a strange group of people. A traditional Salish story tells the Indian view of the meeting. As Chief Three Eagles scouted the land for enemies, he spotted a group of unfamiliar men. Indian men wore blankets as they traveled, but these strangers had no blankets. They looked too pale and tired to be warriors, yet one man seemed to be wearing black paint like a warrior. (It was actually York, Clark's black slave.) An Indian woman and baby accompanied them. This could not be a war party.

Three Eagles returned to his people and described the group. The Indians decided the strangers were most likely defeated warriors. The Indians could easily have overwhelmed the travelers and stolen the Corps' horses and guns, but instead, they met them in peace.

The explorers enjoyed Salish hospitality for two days and traded for some more horses. Then the Indians headed east to join the Shoshone for their annual buffalo hunt, and the Corps of Discovery continued northward down the Bitterroot Valley.

Lewis and Clark planned to cross the Bitterroot Mountains near the north end of the valley, taking the trail used by the Nez Perce tribe when they came east to hunt buffalo and by the Salish when they went west for salmon. The trip through the Bitterroot Valley was easy, but the men knew what lay ahead. The rugged, snowcapped mountains rimmed

The Corps of Discovery could always see the rugged Bitterroot Mountains looming to the west as they traveled along the valley. Today, towns, ranches, and subdivisions dot the landscape.

the valley to the west, in full view. The travelers knew that when they neared the northern end of the valley, they would have to turn west and struggle through those mountains.

On September 9, they reached the spot where present-day Lolo Creek joins the Bitterroot River. Old Toby, their Indian guide, told them this was where they would turn west into the mountains. The expedition camped near the creek at a spot they named Travelers' Rest. On September 10, 1805, the hunters managed to bring in a beaver, four deer, and three grouse. Three Indians from across the mountains also showed up, looking for stolen horses. Talking to them reassured Lewis—if the Indians could cross the mountains, so could he and his men. The Indians told Lewis it would take six days to get across.

The Bitterroot Valley today is dotted with towns, farms, and country homes. It is one of the fastest-growing parts of Montana. Until recently, it was thought that the Travelers' Rest campsite was located close to the banks of the Bitterroot River. Now we know it was actually about a mile up Lolo Creek, on the south side. Like many other places where the Corps of Discovery camped, Travelers' Rest had been used for countless years by the Indians. It provided level land for pitching tepees close to the creek, which supplied water.

Infrared cameras mounted on airplanes have revealed about fifty tepee rings below the surface at Travelers' Rest. Most of the campsite area is a state park, and archaeologists are looking for the location of the campfires and other signs of the Corps of Discovery. The explorers stayed here on their return trip as well, making it one of the most important sites along the Lewis and Clark Trail.

In this painting, Charles M. Russell envisioned the meeting of the Corps of Discovery with the Salish Indians at Ross' Hole. *Montana Historical Society*

The true location of Travelers' Rest was found in 1998. Fortunately, most of the area has never been plowed, so archaeologists are hoping to learn more about the expedition as they study the site.

41

CROSSING THE BITTERROOTS

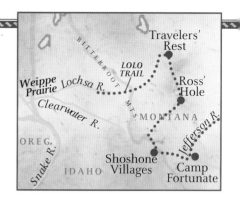

"I have been wet and as cold in every part as I ever was in my life. Indeed, I was at one time fearful my feet would freeze in the thin moccasins I wore. The men are cold and hungry...killed a second colt."

—Clark's Journal, September 16, 1805

Some parts of the Nez Perce Trail, also called the Lolo Trail, are the same today as they were two hundred years ago.

The Bitterroot Mountains remain a formidable barrier to travel. U.S. Highway 12, which roughly follows the route taken by the Corps of Discovery through the mountains, is the only paved highway to cross the Bitterroots. It wasn't completed until 1962. The crest of the Bitterroot Range marks the present boundary between Montana and Idaho, and the land is made up of national forests and wilderness areas.

Crossing these mountains was routine for the Nez Perce and Salish Indians. The Nez Perce came east to hunt buffalo and the Salish went west for salmon. Unfortunately for the Corps of Discovery, the autumn of 1805 was short, and an early winter storm struck just as they headed into the Bitterroots. Rain, hail, and snow pelted the travelers. Clark wrote on September 16, "The mountains which we passed today much worse than yesterday, the last excessively bad and thickly strewn with falling timber...our men and horses much fatigued..."

They ran out of food and had to kill the colts they had brought along. Their guide, Old Toby, got confused on the snowy trail and led the explorers off the Indian trail, which followed a high ridgeline, and took them all the way down to the shores of what we now call the Lochsa River. Toby led them a few miles along the river, struggling over fallen timber, before realizing his error. Then the group had to climb a steep slope to return to the Indian trail. Clark's packhorse slipped and slid down the mountainside, ending up lodged against a tree. Amazingly, the horse was unhurt, but Clark's writing desk was smashed.

From the ridge, about seven thousand feet above sea level, the explorers could see that the mountains went on and on to the west, range after range. How could they possibly cross them?

From the ridgeline trail used by the Nez Perce and Lewis and Clark, mountains stretch in all directions. They look beautiful to us, but they were terrifying to the explorers.

On September 18, Clark went ahead with a few of the men, looking for game. They had no luck with their hunting. But from a high point they could see a prairie to the west, past the mountains. The Bitterroots didn't go on forever. Clark and his men finally left the rugged mountains behind on September 20, when they reached the level ground of Weippe Prairie. There they encountered Nez Perce Indians digging for camas roots, a staple food of the tribe. Most of the Indians had never seen whites before, but they provided the weak and hungry travelers with a feast of roots, salmon, and dried berries. Clark and the others stuffed themselves and then got sick from the unaccustomed diet.

Weippe Prairie, where Clark came upon the Nez Perce, is now farmland. A house stands on the spot where Clark encountered the Indians.

Clark sent one of his men back with food for Lewis and his group. Then Clark visited a nearby Nez Perce village to meet with the chief, whose name was Twisted Hair. The chief drew a map on a white elkskin, showing how the creek they were on entered the Clearwater River, which in turn emptied into the Snake and then into the Columbia. From here on, he said, they could travel by water in canoes.

When Lewis and his men reached the camp, they also became ill from eating the unfamiliar food. Many of them, including Lewis, endured severe vomiting and diarrhea for a week or more.

To the Columbia River

WASH.   MONT.
LOLO TRAIL
Columbia R.
Weippe Prairie   Lochsa R.
BITTERROOT MTS.
Snake R.   Clearwater R.
OREGON
IDAHO

"We set out early in a fine morning and halted at some lodges of

the natives, where we got fish and several dogs. Most of our

people having been accustomed to meat, do not relish the fish,

but prefer dog meat, which, when well cooked, tastes very well."

—Patrick Gass's Journal, October 11, 1805

The Corps of Discovery moved to a timbered site along the Clearwater River, and the men who weren't too sick to work learned from the Indians how to make canoes by burning out the centers of the logs. This method took much less energy than hacking out the wood with axes. The men made six large canoes and one small one from ponderosa pines.

Twisted Hair agreed to take care of the expedition's horses until spring. The Corps of Discovery packed their canoes and left, heading downriver with the current for the first time on their voyage. Lewis had not yet recovered, but it was early October, and the days were getting shorter and shorter. They had to move on.

The men were in a hurry to reach the Pacific. Traveling with the current was a lot quicker than fighting it, but they had to navigate wild rapids in their awkward dugouts. The canoes often turned over, wetting goods and men alike. But still, the explorers chose to take the quicker water route rather than to portage around the rapids.

All along the shores of the Clearwater and

The Nez Perce were famous horse breeders and favored highly colored horses. The tribe is credited with developing the Appaloosa, which is very popular today.

then the Snake River lived Indians belonging to the greater Nez Perce nation. This tribe thrived on the abundant salmon of the Columbia river system and hunted for deer and elk. They raised some of the most beautiful horses in North America, especially spotted ones. The Nez Perce were the only tribe known to practice selective breeding, choosing carefully which stallions to mate with which mares.

In the years after the Lewis and Clark Expedition, as whites took over Indian lands and forced the Indians out, they also took their horses. The once abundant spotted horses of the Nez Perce became rare. In 1938, lovers of these special animals, by then called Appaloosas, formed a club to study their history. Around

The modern city of Lewiston, Idaho, now lies at the junction of the Clearwater and Snake Rivers. From this point on, the once wild Snake River has been tamed by a series of dams.

The Corps of Discovery used dugouts like this one for the trip down to the Pacific Ocean. This replica is at the site of the canoe camp near Orofino, Idaho.

the country, people lucky enough to have Appaloosas joined the club, and the popularity of this hardy breed grew. Today, the beautiful Appaloosa is one of America's most popular horses.

As the Corps of Discovery descended the rivers, they camped and traded with the Indians and shared music and dancing around the campfire at night whenever possible. They were the first white men to enter this region by land, and most of the natives had never even seen any of their kind. Befriending these Indians was especially important for the Corps. No white nation had laid claim to the area yet, but England, Russia, and Spain, in addition to the United States, all wanted it.

On October 16, 1805, the Corps of Discovery reached the Columbia River, just below the present-day cities of Pasco and Kennewick, Washington. They were the first white men to see this part of the Columbia, for traders arriving at the mouth of the river by sea had not yet traveled east of the Cascade Mountains.

For two days, the Corps camped where the Snake River joined the Columbia. Clark took two men in a small canoe and explored for about ten miles up the Columbia. "The number of dead salmon on the shores and floating in the river is incredible," he wrote. He described in his journal how the Indians split the fish and dried them on wooden scaffolds, and he puzzled over where the wood might have come from, since no trees grew nearby.

DESCENDING THE MIGHTY COLUMBIA

"I determined to pass through this place, notwithstanding the horrid

appearance of this agitated gut, swelling, boiling, and whorling

in every direction." —Clark's Journal, October 24, 1805

Today, the Columbia River is tamed by thirteen dams that provide power to millions of people in the Northwest and irrigation water to thousands of farmers. But when the Corps of Discovery descended the river in 1805, no dams blocked the wild river's flow.

On October 23, 1805, the explorers came to an especially dangerous stretch of the river. Beginning at Celilo Falls and continuing for more than fifty-five miles, the Corps of Discovery faced rapid after rapid. In some places, the river passed through narrow channels of churning white water between cliffs three thousand feet high. The explorers portaged the canoes and supplies around the highest falls. They lowered the canoes by ropes and let them bob their way crazily through the lesser rapids.

The next challenge for the explorers was a set of falls later named The Dalles. The landscape in the area was too rugged to portage the heavy dugout canoes, so Lewis and Clark decided to send the men who couldn't swim around the falls by land, carrying the most valuable items such as rifles, ammunition, and journals. Those who could swim braved the rapids in the canoes.

Indians gathered from all around to watch the show. They knew these terrible rapids, and they were convinced the white men could never make it through in their awkward dugouts. But luck was with the explorers, and amazingly, they got through without losing anything.

After one more set of terrifying rapids, the Corps camped on a rocky outcropping they called Fort Rock Camp at what is today the city of The Dalles, Oregon. After the ordeals they had been through, they had to unpack their goods to dry them and repair their battered canoes.

John Day Dam now holds back the Columbia River above Celilo Falls. Farther down the river, the Dalles Dam forms Lake Celilo, which covers the former falls.

The Cascades of the Columbia were the last difficult rapids the Corps had to get past. This 1916 photograph by Asahel Curtis shows the Cascades before Bonneville Dam was built. The dam's waters now cover the Cascades rapids. *Washington State Historical Society, Tacoma*

Interstate Highway 84 and railroad tracks now line the southern shore of the Columbia River.

The final set of rapids came as the Corps of Discovery passed through the Cascade Mountains. This range of volcanoes that includes Mount Rainier and Mount St. Helens divides present-day Washington and Oregon into two very different regions. Storms coming in from the Pacific Ocean encounter the Cascades and drop their moisture as rain on the coastal side, making the cities of Portland, Oregon, and Seattle, Washington, famous for their wet, cool climate. By the time the weather passes over the Cascade Mountains, however, most of the moisture is gone from the clouds, making eastern Washington and Oregon very dry.

It rained on October 30, 1805, as the Corps of Discovery was passing through the Cascades. In his journal for the first few days of November, Clark commented on the thick timber growing near the river, the lingering fog, and the abundant bird life. On November 3, the explorers reached the farthest point upriver that white men had previously ventured. In 1792, Captain George Vancouver had explored this far for the British.

In early November 1805, the Corps was pinned down for days on the shores of the Columbia by a violent storm. Finally, after exploring both the north and south sides of the river, they selected a site for their winter quarters on what is now the Oregon side, a few miles south of the modern town of Astoria. It was located by a small river that emptied into the Columbia. The river is now called the Lewis and Clark River. Good hunting, a spring that provided fresh water, and many trees that could be used to build their fort made the place seem ideal.

Winter at Fort Clatsop

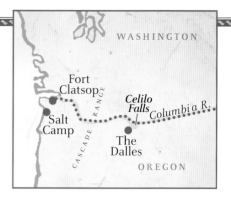

"Rainy & wet. Disagreeable weather. We all moved in to our new fort. The party saluted our officers by each man firing a gun at their quarters at day break this morning. We have nothing to eat but poor elk meat and no salt to season that with but still keep in good spirits as we expect this to be the last winter that we will have to pass in this way."

—John Ordway's Journal, December 25, 1805

Lewis and Clark had their own officers' quarters in the fort. Here they spent many hours, Clark working on his maps and Lewis making detailed entries in his journal.

On December 7, 1805, the men began felling trees to build their fort in the rain. By Christmas Eve, most of them were able to move into their winter quarters. The fort consisted of a sturdy stockade, fifty feet square. On either side of the courtyard were rows of rooms that the men called huts. On one side stood three rooms, each with a fireplace and chimney and crude bunks for the soldiers. Across the way were four rooms. One was for Lewis and Clark, and another for Charbonneau, Sacagawea, and baby Jean Baptiste. The third room was for the sergeant of the guard and his men. The fourth was the meat house.

The winter of 1805–1806 proved to be miserable. Getting thoroughly drenched became a common occurrence. Between December 7, 1805, and March 23, 1806, only twelve days were free of rain, and only six of those were clear. With the only heat coming from the fireplaces, everything stayed damp. By this time, the explorers were wearing mostly leather clothing, which rotted easily. No electricity meant no refrigeration, and the meat spoiled quickly. Even keeping the fire going in the smokehouse was hard, so curing the meat to make it last longer was difficult.

Some scientists today believe the Corps of Discovery was unlucky enough to be in Oregon during a La Niña winter, when the waters of the eastern Pacific Ocean

Fort Clatsop has been reconstructed near its original site. The fort had a heavy gate that was closed every night after it was certain that any visiting Indians had left.

During the early winter, the men made salt at a camp near the ocean using a structure like this. A fire inside the tunnel boiled away the water in the pots on top, leaving behind the salt most of the men craved.

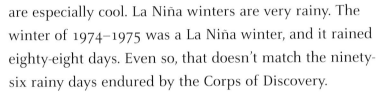

Today, ships such as this cargo vessel on its way to Portland, Oregon, bring steady traffic to the once wild Columbia River.

are especially cool. La Niña winters are very rainy. The winter of 1974–1975 was a La Niña winter, and it rained eighty-eight days. Even so, that doesn't match the ninety-six rainy days endured by the Corps of Discovery.

The men spent much of their time preparing hides and making moccasins for the return journey. By winter's end, they had produced 338 pairs of moccasins, or about 10 pairs per person, hopefully enough for the homeward trek.

During the westward journey, the Corps had run out of salt. In late December, the men found a good location by the sea for a camp where seawater could be boiled to extract the salt. The site was fifteen miles from the fort, which was considered by them a reasonable distance to travel back and forth frequently. They were used to walking every day what we would consider long distances.

They constructed a furnace from rocks and boiled the water in five brass kettles set atop the furnace. Three men at a time manned the furnace, and over the next weeks, they boiled about 1,400 gallons of seawater to produce about 32 gallons of salt.

Lewis and Clark kept busy during the winter catching up on their journals. Lewis expanded many of his descriptions of animals, plants, Indian tribes, geography, and weather. Clark worked on his maps and his geographical data. And, as they did whenever possible, the men copied one another's journals in case some got lost.

On March 23, 1806, the Corps of Discovery left Fort Clatsop, eager to return home. Traveling up the Columbia was difficult both because of bad weather and trouble with the Indians. The Americans were relieved to leave the river during the fourth week of April and head overland back into Nez Perce country.

"That icy barrier which separates me from my friends and country,

from all which makes life estimable, is yet white with the snow,

which is many feet deep." —*Clark's Journal, May 17, 1806*

After reaching the Nez Perce villages they had visited on the way west in early May, the travelers learned from the Indians that the winter had been especially harsh and snow still blocked the mountains. Travel through them would be impossible for at least another three weeks. The Americans set up camp near the Indian villages on the banks of the Clearwater River to wait.

During the earlier stay with the Nez Perce, Clark had successfully treated some members of the tribe for their ailments. Medicines of the day were very primitive, but Clark seemed to have a knack for making the best use of what treatments he had. Now the Indians wanted more of his doctoring and traded roots and dogs for it, which helped feed the explorers. Since the Corps of Discovery had almost run out of trade goods, the payments for Clark's treatments were vital to the group's food supply.

People always enjoy athletic competition, and while they waited for the snow to melt, the Americans amused themselves in contests with Indian men. They held a shooting match. The Americans used their guns and the Indians shot arrows from the backs of galloping horses. Each group impressed the other.

They also raced horses. Lewis was very taken with the Nez Perce horses and wrote in his journal, "several of those horses would be thought fleet in the U. States." The Nez Perce were spectacular horsemen. "It is astonishing to see these people

When Clark first saw camas in bloom on June 12, 1806, he wrote "at a short distance it resembles a lake of fine clear water. So complete is this deception that on first sight I could have sworn it was water."

50

ride down those steep hills, which they do at full speed," wrote Lewis.

June arrived, and still snow blanketed the mountains. The Americans became more and more restless. Finally, on June 10, they moved their camp up to Weippe Prairie, closer to the mountains they would soon have to cross.

Weippe Prairie was abloom with beautiful blue camas flowers. "The quawmash [camas] is now in bloom and from the color of its bloom at a short distance it resembles a lake of fine clear water," wrote Clark. Spring had come—the mountains must be passable by now, the men thought.

The Indians had warned the expedition leaders that it was still too early to cross the mountains, but the Americans could wait no longer. On June 15, they headed into the Bitterroots without Indian guides. Two days later, as they climbed higher, they encountered snow twelve to fifteen feet deep. The snow was firm enough that they could travel on top of it, but there was no food for the horses.

Lewis and Clark were impatient to get under way, and they left the Nez Perce, although the Indians said it was still too early. The explorers encountered deep snow and weren't able to continue without help from the Nez Perce.

They knew it could only get worse if they continued, so they retreated to a lower altitude where there was grass for the horses. They sent two men back to persuade some Indians to guide them through the Bitterroots. After five nervous days, the two men returned on June 23 with three Indian guides willing to take them through the mountains in trade for two rifles.

The Indians knew the mountains so well that they were able to pace the journey perfectly, arriving almost every day to a place where the horses could graze. Only once did the horses have to go hungry. On June 30, they arrived once again at Travelers' Rest. With the Nez Perce to guide them, they had crossed the snowy Bitterroots in just six days.

"At about 12 o'clock we arrived in site of St. Louis, fired three rounds as
we approached the town, and landed opposite the center of the town.
The people gathered on the shore and huzzahed three cheers.
We unloaded the canoes and carried the baggage all up to a storehouse
in town. We intend to return to our native homes to see our
parents once more as we have been so long from them."
—John Ordway's Journal, September 23, 1806

After three days at Travelers' Rest, repacking and finalizing their homeward routes, the Corps of Discovery split into two groups. Lewis took nine men and seventeen horses with him to explore a shortcut across the Continental Divide to Great Falls. Clark and the rest of the group retraced their steps as far as the headwaters of the Jefferson River, where they would split into two more groups.

The return journey allowed the Corps of Discovery to explore new territory. Clark and his group descended the Yellowstone River, reveling in an abundance of wild fruit and wildlife. "…for me to give an estimate of the different species [meaning number of individual animals] of wild animals on this river would be increditable. I shall therefore be silent on the subject," he wrote on July 24.

On July 25, they reached a hill with sandstone cliffs that Clark named after Sacagawea's son. Clark carved his name and the date into the soft stone. The sandstone outcrop is still called Pompeys Pillar. Today, Clark's signature, the only written mark that has survived along the trail, is protected by a plastic cover.

On August 3, 1806, Clark reached the Missouri River and camped at the same

Clark and his men used a canoe like this to explore the Yellowstone River on the return trip.

The view from Pompeys Pillar today shows farms and croplands instead of herds of the abundant wildlife viewed by Clark in 1806.

Clark carved his name into the soft sandstone of Pompeys Pillar, the only physical sign left by the Corps of Discovery that survives today.

spot where the Corps of Discovery had made camp on April 26, 1805. He was supposed to meet Lewis and his men here. But the mosquitoes tortured everyone, especially Pomp, so much that Clark left a note for Lewis and continued down the river. Soon the rest of his own group rejoined them.

Finally, on August 12, Lewis and his men caught up. They had plenty of stories to share. Lewis and three men had split off to explore the Marias River. They had a run-in with some Blackfeet warriors and had killed one of them. Galloping away as fast as possible, traveling sixty-three miles before even resting, they continued on until two in the morning. Luckily, the four men met up with the rest of their group just as they reached the Missouri River. They quickly packed their gear into the canoes, let the horses loose, and headed down the river. Then, on August 11, Lewis and Private Cruzatte went elk hunting in a willow thicket. Cruzatte accidentally shot Lewis in the left thigh.

Because of the painful wound, Lewis had to continue the voyage lying on his stomach in the canoe. The explorers dropped Charbonneau and his family off at the Mandan villages and stopped at Sergeant Floyd's grave to pay their respects. Finally, on September 20, they arrived at the small settlement of La Charette just north of St. Louis. The town's people were amazed to see them. They had been gone so long that many had given them up for dead. When they arrived in St. Louis three days later, they received a heroes' welcome.

Once they reached St. Louis, the Corps of Discovery quickly dispersed. Some of the men were anxious to head back into the wilderness to seek their fortune in the fur trade. Others were anxious to return to their families. Each man except the slave, York, received three hundred and twenty acres of land and the pay that had accumulated during the journey.

AFTERMATH

"I received, my dear Sir, with unspeakable joy, your letter of Sep. 23 announcing the return of yourself, Capt. Clark & your party in good health to St. Louis. The unknown scenes in which you were engaged, & the length of time without hearing of you had begun to be felt awfully. This letter's only object is to assure you of what you already know, my constant affection for you & the joy with which all your friends here will receive you."

—Jefferson's letter to Lewis, October 26, 1806

Lewis sat down to write a report to President Jefferson immediately. The last correspondence from Lewis had been from Fort Mandan, almost a year and a half earlier. The most important part of the journey had occurred since then. Lewis reluctantly told Jefferson about the difficult passage over the Rocky Mountains—three hundred and forty miles, one hundred and forty of which were steep and difficult. Jefferson had to give up his dream of a water route across the continent.

Lewis arrived in Washington to visit with the president on December 28, 1806. They hadn't seen each other for three and a half years, and they had much to talk about. Unfortunately, no record remains of their conversation.

The tales of adventure and natural riches the men brought home helped inspire more and more settlement and exploration in the Louisiana Territory. A fifth of the Corps of Discovery returned to the West and made their lives there. In 1818, Louisiana became the first state west of the Mississippi River, and in 1822, Missouri was granted statehood, the first state of what was truly the West. The United States was on its way to becoming a powerful nation.

Today, the area around the Platte River in Nebraska, past which Lewis and Clark traveled, is a checkerboard of farmland, not a prairie teeming with wildlife.

William Clark became governor of the Missouri Territory from 1813 to 1820. He married his young cousin Julia Hancock. She had been only twelve years old when the expedition began, but Clark had already had his eye on her. In May of 1805, he had named a river after Julia, who appears to have also used the name Judith. He called it Judith's River, and today it is the Judith River. It is one of the few rivers named by Lewis and Clark that retains the name they gave.

Clark was also in charge of Indian affairs in the West and did what he could to

help the Indians receive fair treatment from the U.S. government. After Sacagawea died in 1812, Clark took in both her son, Jean Baptiste, and his little sister and raised them.

Clark was a master mapmaker. His map of North America filled in the huge blanks that appeared in maps before the expedition.

Clark sympathized with the Indians, but he refused to honor his slave York's request for his freedom after the expedition. York felt he deserved freedom as a reward for the vital services he performed for the Corps of Discovery. He wanted to join his wife, also a slave, who belonged to someone in Kentucky. But the ingrained attitudes of a slaveholder died hard. Clark wrote to his brother, "I did wish to do well by him, but as he has got such a notion about freedom and his immense services, that I do not expect he will be of much service to me again." The relationship between Clark and York continued to deteriorate until Clark gave him "a severe trouncing" in 1809. Finally, in 1811, Clark gave York his freedom. No one is certain what happened next, but York probably went on to run a freight wagon company in Kentucky and Tennessee. According to Clark, the business failed. York then tried to return to St. Louis to be with Clark but died of cholera before he got there. Some people believe he went West instead and lived with the Crow Indians. Clark died in 1838.

Jefferson named Meriwether Lewis governor of the Louisiana Territory. Partly because of his duties in this difficult job, Lewis did not follow through on getting the journals of the expedition published right away. He died in 1809 from gunshot wounds he received while on his way to Washington. His death is a mystery to this day. Some people believe Lewis was killed by a bandit. Others, who cite Lewis's tendency toward depression and his numerous financial difficulties after returning, as well as his disappointing personal life, think he shot himself.

The Corps of Discovery would never have completed its journey without the help of Indians along the way. The Mandan and Hidatsa provided them with food and information about what lay ahead during the winter of 1804–1805. The Shoshone and Salish supplied horses. The Nez Perce fed the explorers when they stumbled out of the Bitterroot Mountains near death from starvation. The Nez Perce also taught them the Indian way to make canoes and took care of their horses for the winter.

As the Corps of Discovery descended the Columbia River, tribes along the way traded food such as salmon and dogs for the expedition's goods. During the winter at Fort Clatsop, the coastal Indians traded with the explorers and introduced them to new foods.

Indians all across North America have suffered the takeover of their lands and diseases brought by the whites. Many tribes were reduced to small numbers, and some have disappeared completely. Most of those that survive live on reservations, often away from their traditional lands or occupying only a small portion of the lands they once roamed freely.

The Sioux, who controlled much of the commerce on the plains and who fought many battles with the whites, including the Battle of Little Bighorn, are still battling with the U.S. government. In 1868, the United States signed a treaty setting aside the Black Hills of what is now South Dakota "for the absolute and undisturbed use and occupancy of the Sioux." But after gold was discovered in the region, Congress took it back in 1877. The government wants to compensate the Sioux with a financial settlement, but the Indians refuse. They want their land. The Sioux live on reservations in North and South Dakota, Minnesota, Nebraska, and Montana.

In 1855, the Nez Perce signed away some of their lands in exchange for a guarantee that they could keep the rest of it. The whites, however, soon violated the treaty and took more Nez Perce land. In this drawing, the Nez Perce are shown arriving at Walla Walla, now in Washington State, for the treaty signing. *Washington State Historical Society, Tacoma, Washington*

Today, the Mandan, Hidatsa, and Arikara share the Fort Berthold Reservation in North Dakota. A smallpox epidemic in 1837 almost killed off the Hidatsa, and all but 125 Mandan also died in the epidemic. The three tribes have cooperated in setting up the Three Affiliated Tribes Museum on their reservation at New Town, North Dakota.

The Shoshone were once one of the widest-ranging tribes in North America, living in what are now the states of Nevada, Idaho, Utah, Wyoming, and California. Today, they are scattered among reservations in all these states except Wyoming. Some are shared with other tribes. The Lemhi Shoshone, Sacagawea's branch of the tribe, still lives in Idaho, and includes some direct descendants of her brother, Cameahwait. The Sacajawea Interpretive, Cultural, and Education Center in Salmon, Idaho, helps give the Indian viewpoint of the Lewis and Clark Expedition and the life of Sacagawea.

The Salish Indians were given a reservation in the Bitterroot Valley at first, but later the land was taken away from them, and they were forced to move to the Flathead Reservation in the Mission Valley of Montana, which they share with the Kootenai Indians today.

Tribes that lived along the Columbia River have been greatly reduced and have lost the most important part of their economy—salmon. The Clatsop, who lived at

All along the Columbia River and the northern Pacific coast, the Indians depended on salmon for their survival. The Columbia River tribes dried salmon on wooden racks similar to those seen in this photo taken near Port Angeles, Washington, in the early 1900s. *Bert Kellogg Collection, North Olympic Library*

Charles M. Russell painted *Lewis and Clark on the Lower Columbia* in 1905. The watercolor painting shows the Indians in ceremonial dress, probably from a later date than the Lewis and Clark Expedition. The Indians wouldn't have worn such clothing while greeting strangers in a canoe, in any case. The painting shows the elegant canoes made by these people. *Amon Carter Museum, Fort Worth, Texas, Acc. No. 1961.195*

the mouth of the river and interacted regularly with the Corps of Discovery, were a tribe of the Chinook people, who now share a reservation near Oakville, Washington, with the Chehalis Indians.

Perhaps the saddest fate of the Indians belongs to the Nez Perce. Throughout their interactions with whites, these people prided themselves on being peaceful. They were proud that they had never killed a white man. The whites betrayed them anyway, trying to force a band of Nez Perce to leave their home in the Wallowa Valley in northwest Oregon and move to the Nez Perce Reservation at Lapwai, in present-day Idaho.

This demand was too much for some young Nez Perce warriors, who killed a number of the abusive whites. Thus began a series of battles as the Indians fled toward Canada. The U.S. Cavalry pursued them for 1,700 miles to within 30 miles of the Canadian border. There, the Indian leader Chief Joseph surrendered and gave a speech that ended, "From where the sun now stands, I will fight no more forever."

Today, Indians all across America are improving their lives. Many have established their own schools, where they can teach their languages and traditions along with standard subjects. Many Indians leave their reservations to get a college education. Some continue into fields such as law and use their skills to help the tribes in their battles with the government. On the reservations, tribes are finding ways of making economic progress by building casinos, hotels, and museums to educate the public or developing natural resources such as oil or power from the wind. Some tribes are reviving their treasured traditions, including bringing buffalo and Indian horses back to their reservations.

Powwows, where Indians from different tribes compete in dancing, rodeos, and games, are becoming more and more popular in both the United States and Canada. Here, the late war-dance chief of the Flathead Nation, John Peter Paul, dances at the annual powwow held on the Flathead Indian Reservation in Arlee, Montana, home of the Salish and Kootenai tribes.

There are many fine books available on the Lewis and Clark Expedition. I am the author of two other books on the subject: *Animals Along the Trail with Lewis and Clark* (New York: Clarion, 2002), which describes the animals they found, including information on how the animals lived before European-American settlement, and *Plants Along the Trail with Lewis and Clark* (New York: Clarion, 2003), which discusses the plants Lewis collected and described. *The Incredible Journey of Lewis and Clark,* by Rhoda Blumberg (Magnolia, MA: Peter Smith Publishers, 1999), is an award-winning book for young people that gives an overall view of the expedition.

For those who want to explore parts of the trail themselves, *Along the Trail with Lewis and Clark,* 2nd edition, by Barbara Fifer and Vicky Soderberg (Helena, MT: Montana Magazine/Farcountry Press, 2002), has lots of quotations from the journals and excellent maps prepared by Joseph Musselman as well as abundant information about sites along the way.

For those who explore the Internet, "Lewis & Clark on the Information Superhighway" (**http://www.lcarchive.org/fulllist.html**) provides links to every site on the Web that concerns Lewis and Clark. A couple of especially good ones are "Discovering Lewis and Clark" (**http://www.lewis~clark.org**) and the official home of the Lewis and Clark Trail Heritage Foundation, Inc. (**http://www.lewisandclark.org/**). I have information about my own experiences along the trail on my Web site, **http://www.dorothyhinshawpatent.com**.

INDEX

Page numbers in *italics* refer to maps and illustrations.